DAY AND NIGHT IN THE

Savanna

by Mary Boone

PEBBLE
a capstone imprint

Published by Pebble, an imprint of Capstone.
1710 Roe Crest Drive, North Mankato, Minnesota 56003
capstonepub.com

Library of Congress Cataloging-in-Publication Data is on file with the Library of Congress.
ISBN: 9781663976901 (hardcover)
ISBN: 9781666327878 (paperback)
ISBN: 9781666327885 (ebook PDF)

Summary: Spend a day and night in the savanna! Learn about this grassy habitat through the interesting animals that call it home. Nibble a breakfast of sky-high leaves with a giraffe. Then go on a high-speed hunt with a cheetah. At sunset, build towering mounds with termites. After dark, prowl for prey with a pack of hyenas. What will tomorrow bring in the savanna?

Image Credits
iStockphoto: 1001slide, Cover (savanna), 1, 25ehaag6, Cover (giraffe), 1; Mighty Media, Inc.: 20, 21; Shutterstock: Benjamin B, 17, Dave Montreuil, 9, EcoPrint, 15, kavram, 18, Kelsey Green, 19, Kobus Peche, 16, Linda Marie Caldwell, 13, Pavel Krasensky, 12, Pearl Media, 14, PHOTOCREO Michal Bednarek, 5, Stu Porter, 11, thoron, 8, tonyzhao120, 7

Editorial Credits
Jessica Rusick, editor, media researcher; Kelly Doudna, designer, production specialist

All internet sites appearing in back matter were available and accurate when this book was sent to press.

Printed and bound in the USA. 4608

Table of Contents

Words in **bold** are in the glossary.

What Are Savannas?

Savannas are grassy **habitats**. They have scattered **shrubs** and trees. Savannas are hot during the day. They cool down at night.

Savannas are found in Africa, South America, Asia, and Australia. They are home to many animals. Some come out during the day. Others come out at night.

An African savanna

Morning

The sun rises over an African savanna. A giraffe eats while it is still cool. It plucks leaves from the tops of trees. Its long neck and tongue help it reach.

Giraffes are the world's tallest **mammals**. They spend much of their time eating. Some giraffes eat 75 pounds (34 kilograms) of food each day.

Giraffe

Noon

The noon sun is hot. A thirsty elephant circles a baobab tree. Baobab trees have water in their trunks. The elephant scrapes off the tree's bark with its **tusks**. Then, it makes a hole in the tree. The elephant reaches inside to get the water.

Baobab tree

Elephant

Late Afternoon

A cheetah chases a gazelle. The big cat can run 70 miles (113 kilometers) per hour! The cheetah knocks the gazelle down. It bites the animal with its teeth.

Many big cats hunt at night. But cheetahs can't see well in the dark. They hunt during the day. Cheetahs also hunt in daylight to avoid other **predators**.

A cheetah chasing a gazelle

Evening

A termite mound towers over the savanna. Termites built the mound from dirt, spit, and poop. Some mounds are more than 30 feet (9 meters) tall!

Termites

A leopard on a termite mound

Termites live in a nest below the
mound. At sunset, they prepare to leave
the nest. They will gather wood to eat.

Night

The air cools. A cape porcupine sniffs for food. It finds an animal bone. The porcupine carries the bone to its **burrow**. It chews the bone to get **minerals**.

Cape porcupine

Springhare

A springhare digs for roots and seeds.
Its large eyes help it see in the dark. The
springhare hears a noise. It leaps away
using its strong back legs.

Late Night

Shrieks and whoops **echo** across the savanna. A hyena clan is on the move. Hyenas sometimes eat animals killed by other predators. They also hunt.

The clan spots a gemsbok separated from its herd. The hyenas chase the gemsbok. They take the animal down together.

Gemsbok

Hyena

Dawn

The sun rises. An aardvark has spent the night searching for ants and termites. Now it returns to rest in its burrow.

Other animals wake. Kingfisher birds whistle and chirp. Zebras eat grass. Another day on the savanna has begun.

Kingfisher

Aardvark

Giraffe Activity

What You Need:

- yellow construction paper
- cardboard tube
- glue stick
- brown construction paper
- pencil
- scissors
- black marker

What You Do:

1. Wrap a sheet of yellow construction paper around a cardboard tube. Glue the seam.

2. Tear a sheet of brown construction paper into small pieces. These are the giraffe's spots.

3. Glue the spots onto the cardboard tube. This is the giraffe's neck.

4. Draw an oval on yellow paper. Add ears and two small horns to the oval. This is the giraffe's head.

5. Cut out the giraffe's head.

6. Draw eyes and nostrils on the head with black marker.

7. Glue the head to one end of the cardboard tube. Put on a puppet show with your giraffe!

Glossary

burrow (BUHR-oh)—a tunnel or hole in the ground made or used by an animal

echo (EK-oh)—to repeat over and over again

habitat (HAB-uh-tat)—the natural place and conditions in which a plant or animal lives

mammal (MAM-uhl)—a warm-blooded animal that breathes air; mammals have hair or fur; female mammals feed milk to their young

mineral (MIN-ur-uhl)—a natural chemical that animals need to stay healthy

predator (PRED-uh-tur)—an animal that hunts other animals for food

shrub (SHRUHB)—a plant or bush with woody stems that branch out near the ground

tusk (TUHSK)—a long, pointed tooth that sticks out when the mouth is closed

Read More

Jaycox, Jaclyn. *Cheetahs*. Mankato, MN: Capstone, 2020.

Latham, Donna. *Biomes: Discover the Earth's Ecosystems with Environmental Science Activities for Kids*. White River Junction, VT: Nomad Press, 2019.

Platt, John and Moira Rose Donohue. *Lions & Cheetahs & Rhinos OH MY!: Animal Artwork by Children in Sub-Saharan Africa*. Ann Arbor, MI: Sleeping Bear Press, 2020.

Internet Sites

DK Find Out!—African Savanna
dkfindout.com/us/animals-and-nature/habitats-and-ecosystems/african-savanna/

National Geographic Kids—Save Our Savannahs!
natgeokids.com/uk/home-is-good/savannah-habitat/

San Diego Zoo Kids—Spectacular Savannas
kids.sandiegozoo.org/stories/spectacular-savannas

Index

About the Author

Mary Boone has written more than 60 nonfiction books for young readers, ranging from biographies to craft guides. Mary lives in Tacoma, Washington, where she shares an office with an Airedale Terrier named Ruthie Bader.